HERO
on a
MISSION
Planner

HERO
on a
MISSION

Planner

DONALD MILLER

HarperCollins
Leadership

An Imprint of HarperCollins

Published by HarperCollins Leadership, an imprint of HarperCollins Focus LLC.

ISBN 978-1-4002-2802-7 (eBook)
ISBN 978-1-4002-3785-2 (TP)

Library of Congress Cataloging-in-Publication Data
Library of Congress Cataloging-in-Publication application has been submitted.

Printed in South Korea
22 23 24 25 26 IMS 10 9 8 7 6 5 4 3 2 1

Explore how this planner can be used for your entire team or association:

Table of Contents

Your Life Plan

Your Morning Ritual and Daily Planner Pages

Foreword for the Hero on a Mission Planner

I DON'T THINK ANY OF us should trust fate to write the story of our lives. Fate is a terrible writer. Instead, we should shape the direction of our lives by performing a simple morning ritual.

Filling out the Hero on a Mission Planner (based on the book *Hero on a Mission*) is a morning ritual that will help you gain agency over your life, end a victim mindset, and usher in a deep sense of meaning.

Many people feel as though they are sitting in the theater of their mind, waiting for a story to show up on the screen. But after the cultural scripts of childhood, school, college, marriage, and raising children are over, culture stops handing us scripts. It's up to us, then, to write a new story for our lives. And the earlier we learn to do this, the more agency we gain, and the more we get to decide whether or not we find our lives interesting.

The term I use to describe the restlessness of sitting in the theater of our minds, waiting for something to happen, is the *narrative void*. Losing interest in our own story—mainly because our story isn't interesting—is the sad fate of many. But this does not have to be the case.

We can fight the narrative void by intentionally designing a story for our lives and waking up each day to move that story forward. When we do this, we experience a deep sense of meaning.

For a long time I believed "meaning" was a philosophical idea that you experienced only when you agreed with a set of beliefs. I no longer believe this is true. In fact, I don't think meaning can be experienced by believing a set of ideas at all. I believe meaning is something we experience in motion. Meaning requires action.

This planner will guide you through a morning ritual that will do more than make you productive. It will help you design and live a life in which you experience meaning.

According to the Viennese psychologist Viktor Frankl, we experience meaning when we intentionally do three things:

1. We involve ourselves in a deed or project that requires our attention.
2. We accept challenges and suffering as part of our lives and realize that, while painful or annoying, challenges and suffering also offer us the ability to transform into better versions of ourselves.
3. We gain an interest in people, art, or nature. Essentially, we are no longer entirely consumed with ourselves and, to some degree, find an interest outside ourselves.

This formula for meaning is pragmatic and simple, but it works. When we go through the steps of the Hero on a Mission Planner, we find ourselves swallowed up in a story of our own making. This in turn moves us into narrative traction.

Narrative traction happens when we are so interested in the story of our lives that we are eager to get up every morning and put a little something on the plot.

What so many of us are missing in life is a deep experience of meaning. My hope is that the morning ritual you perform by filling out this planner invites you into a story of your own making, a story that delivers more than productivity and success and that delivers a deep experience of meaning.

Sincerely,
Donald Miller

Your Life Plan

My Eulogy

My Life Plan Ten-Year Vision

If a movie was made about your life this year, what would it be called?

Age

Career

-
-
-

Health

-
-
-

Family

-
-
-

Friends

-
-
-

Spiritual

-
-
-
-

2 things I try to do every day

-
-

2 things I don't do

-
-

Notes

My Life Plan Five-Year Vision

If a movie was made about your life this year, what would it be called?

____

Age

____

Career

- ______________________
- ______________________
- ______________________

Health

- ______________________
- ______________________
- ______________________

Family

- ______________________
- ______________________
- ______________________

Friends

- ______________________
- ______________________
- ______________________

Spiritual

- ______________________
- ______________________
- ______________________
- ______________________

2 things I try to do every day

- ______________________
- ______________________

2 things I don't do

- ______________________
- ______________________

Notes

My Life Plan One-Year Vision

If a movie was made about your life this year, what would it be called?

Age

Career

Health

Family

Friends

Spiritual

2 things I try to do every day

2 things I don't do

Goal name	Completion date

Describe this goal

Why does this goal matter to you?

Goal partners *(optional)*	1	2	3
Milestones	1	2	3

Daily sacrifices

Repetition record

Goal name	Completion date

Describe this goal

Why does this goal matter to you?

Goal partners *(optional)*	1	2	3
Milestones	1	2	3

Daily sacrifices

Repetition record												

Goal name	Completion date

Describe this goal

____

____

____

____

____

Why does this goal matter to you?

____

____

____

____

____

Goal partners *(optional)*	1	2	3
Milestones	1	2	3

Daily sacrifices

____

____

____

____

____

Repetition record												

Your Morning Ritual and Daily Planner Pages

“My morning ritual gives me clarity about what my story is about, why it’s important, and what I need to do that day to put something on the plot. With that clarity, I start my day.”

From *Hero on a Mission*

DO YOU HAVE a morning ritual that centers you and reminds you what your personal story is about?

Morning Ritual

My ritual goes like this:

1. *I read my eulogy.*
Yes, I've already written my eulogy, and every morning, I read it. I got this idea from Stephen Covey. It benefits me to read my eulogy because it helps me start with the end in mind.

2. *I read my ten-year, five-year, and one-year visions for my life.*
I've included three pages that, in a way, set my life in motion to become the sort of person I read about in my eulogy. Not unlike how a professional golfer lines up her putt to roll over a line of specks on the green so her ball finds the hole, I use my one-, five-, and ten-year vision pages to direct my life at a closer range.

3. *I read my goal-setting worksheets.*
I read about the three goals I am currently working on. Each serves as a sort of brick in the wall for my overall life plan. I only give myself three goals at a time because it's hard for a human brain to prioritize more than three projects.

4. *I fill out my daily planner page.*

I created this page more than ten years ago but kept it mostly private until I decided to write this book. I credit this planner page with keeping me focused and driving a moderate level of intensity. If I were to reverse-engineer any success I've achieved, I'd credit this tool.

Hero on a Mission Daily Planner

Date

My Morning Ritual

- [ ] I've read my eulogy
- [ ] I've reviewed my vision worksheets
- [ ] I've reviewed my goals

Primary task one

Primary task two

Primary task three

Secondary tasks

- [ ]
- [ ]
- [ ]
- [ ]
- [ ]

If you could live this day again, what would you do differently this time?

-
-
-

What am I grateful for today?

-
-
-
-

Appointments

:
:
:
:
:
:
:
:
:
:
:
:
:

"The term I now use to describe the restlessness of sitting in the theater of our minds waiting for something to happen is *narrative void*. No longer being interested in your own story, mainly because the story isn't interesting: that's how many people live. And it's sad."

From *Hero on a Mission*

NEARLY 10 PERCENT of the American workforce has quit their jobs in the last few months. What if people aren't just tired of their work? What if they're tired of their lives? What if this is an existential crisis? What they need is to design a new story for their lives. A new story involves a great deal more than a new career.

Hero on a Mission Daily Planner

Date

My Morning Ritual

- [ ] I've read my eulogy
- [ ] I've reviewed my vision worksheets
- [ ] I've reviewed my goals

Primary task one

Primary task two

Primary task three

Secondary tasks

- [ ]
- [ ]
- [ ]
- [ ]
- [ ]

If you could live this day again, what would you do differently this time?

-
-
-

What am I grateful for today?

-
-
-
-

Appointments

	:
	:
	:
	:
	:
	:
	:
	:
	:
	:
	:
	:
	:

Hero on a Mission Daily Planner

Date

My Morning Ritual

- [ ] I've read my eulogy
- [ ] I've reviewed my vision worksheets
- [ ] I've reviewed my goals

Primary task one

Primary task two

Primary task three

Secondary tasks

- [ ]
- [ ]
- [ ]
- [ ]
- [ ]

If you could live this day again, what would you do differently this time?

-
-
-

What am I grateful for today?

-
-
-
-

Appointments

Hero on a Mission Daily Planner

Date

My Morning Ritual

- ☐ I've read my eulogy
- ☐ I've reviewed my vision worksheets
- ☐ I've reviewed my goals

Primary task one

Primary task two

Primary task three

Secondary tasks

- ☐
- ☐
- ☐
- ☐
- ☐

If you could live this day again, what would you do differently this time?

-
-
-

What am I grateful for today?

-
-
-
-

Appointments

	:
	:
	:
	:
	:
	:
	:
	:
	:
	:
	:
	:
	:

Hero on a Mission Daily Planner

Date

My Morning Ritual

- [ ] I've read my eulogy
- [ ] I've reviewed my vision worksheets
- [ ] I've reviewed my goals

Primary task one

Primary task two

Primary task three

Secondary tasks

- [ ]
- [ ]
- [ ]
- [ ]
- [ ]

If you could live this day again, what would you do differently this time?

What am I grateful for today?

Appointments

Hero on a Mission Daily Planner

Date

My Morning Ritual

- [ ] I've read my eulogy
- [ ] I've reviewed my vision worksheets
- [ ] I've reviewed my goals

Primary task one

Primary task two

Primary task three

Secondary tasks

- [ ]
- [ ]
- [ ]
- [ ]
- [ ]

If you could live this day again, what would you do differently this time?

-
-
-

What am I grateful for today?

-
-
-
-

Appointments

	:
	:
	:
	:
	:
	:
	:
	:
	:
	:
	:
	:
	:

"For a long time I believed 'meaning' was a philosophical idea that you experienced only when you agreed with a set of beliefs. I no longer believe this is true. In fact, I don't think meaning can be experienced by believing a set of ideas at all. Instead, I believe meaning is something you experience in motion. . . . Meaning requires action."

From *Hero on a Mission*

I DON'T BELIEVE you can experience meaning by studying meaning, any more than I think you can experience love by studying the brain chemistry that brings about feelings of love. To experience meaning, you have to step into a meaningful story. You have to take action.

Hero on a Mission Daily Planner

Date

My Morning Ritual

- [ ] I've read my eulogy
- [ ] I've reviewed my vision worksheets
- [ ] I've reviewed my goals

Primary task one

Primary task two

Primary task three

Secondary tasks

- [ ]
- [ ]
- [ ]
- [ ]
- [ ]

If you could live this day again, what would you do differently this time?

-
-
-

What am I grateful for today?

-
-
-
-

Appointments

:
:
:
:
:
:
:
:
:
:
:
:
:

Hero on a Mission Daily Planner

Date

My Morning Ritual

- [ ] I've read my eulogy
- [ ] I've reviewed my vision worksheets
- [ ] I've reviewed my goals

Primary task one

Primary task two

Primary task three

Secondary tasks

- [ ]
- [ ]
- [ ]
- [ ]
- [ ]

If you could live this day again, what would you do differently this time?

-
-
-

What am I grateful for today?

-
-
-
-

Appointments

Hero on a Mission Daily Planner

Date

My Morning Ritual

- [ ] I've read my eulogy
- [ ] I've reviewed my vision worksheets
- [ ] I've reviewed my goals

Primary task one

Primary task two

Primary task three

Secondary tasks

- [ ]
- [ ]
- [ ]
- [ ]
- [ ]

If you could live this day again, what would you do differently this time?

-
-
-

What am I grateful for today?

-
-
-
-

Appointments

	:
	:
	:
	:
	:
	:
	:
	:
	:
	:
	:
	:
	:
	:

Hero on a Mission Daily Planner

Date

My Morning Ritual

- [ ] I've read my eulogy
- [ ] I've reviewed my vision worksheets
- [ ] I've reviewed my goals

Primary task one

Primary task two

Primary task three

Secondary tasks

- [ ]
- [ ]
- [ ]
- [ ]
- [ ]

If you could live this day again, what would you do differently this time?

-
-
-

What am I grateful for today?

-
-
-
-

Appointments

:
:
:
:
:
:
:
:
:
:
:
:
:

Hero on a Mission Daily Planner

Date

My Morning Ritual

- [ ] I've read my eulogy
- [ ] I've reviewed my vision worksheets
- [ ] I've reviewed my goals

Primary task one

Primary task two

Primary task three

Secondary tasks

- [ ]
- [ ]
- [ ]
- [ ]
- [ ]

If you could live this day again, what would you do differently this time?

-
-
-

What am I grateful for today?

-
-
-
-

Appointments

:
:
:
:
:
:
:
:
:
:
:
:
:

Hero on a Mission Daily Planner

Date

My Morning Ritual

- [ ] I've read my eulogy
- [ ] I've reviewed my vision worksheets
- [ ] I've reviewed my goals

Primary task one

Primary task two

Primary task three

Secondary tasks

- [ ]
- [ ]
- [ ]
- [ ]
- [ ]

If you could live this day again, what would you do differently this time?

-
-
-

What am I grateful for today?

-
-
-
-

Appointments

Hero on a Mission Daily Planner

Date

My Morning Ritual

- [ ] I've read my eulogy
- [ ] I've reviewed my vision worksheets
- [ ] I've reviewed my goals

Primary task one

Primary task two

Primary task three

Secondary tasks

- [ ]
- [ ]
- [ ]
- [ ]
- [ ]

If you could live this day again, what would you do differently this time?

-
-
-

What am I grateful for today?

-
-
-
-

Appointments

"Many people live in an existential vacuum without realizing they can easily experience meaning again. They just have to get a little story going."

From *Hero on a Mission*

TO LIVE A story, identify something meaningful (and specific) that you want in life. Pursue that thing even though there may be challenges. Let the challenges transform you into a better version of yourself. This is the formula for experiencing a deep sense of meaning.

Hero on a Mission Daily Planner

Date

My Morning Ritual

- [ ] I've read my eulogy
- [ ] I've reviewed my vision worksheets
- [ ] I've reviewed my goals

Primary task one

Primary task two

Primary task three

Secondary tasks

- [ ]
- [ ]
- [ ]
- [ ]
- [ ]

If you could live this day again, what would you do differently this time?

-
-
-

What am I grateful for today?

-
-
-
-

Appointments

Hero on a Mission Daily Planner

Date

My Morning Ritual

- [ ] I've read my eulogy
- [ ] I've reviewed my vision worksheets
- [ ] I've reviewed my goals

Primary task one

Primary task two

Primary task three

Secondary tasks

- [ ]
- [ ]
- [ ]
- [ ]
- [ ]

If you could live this day again, what would you do differently this time?

-
-
-

What am I grateful for today?

-
-
-
-

Appointments

Hero on a Mission Daily Planner

Date

My Morning Ritual

- [ ] I've read my eulogy
- [ ] I've reviewed my vision worksheets
- [ ] I've reviewed my goals

Primary task one

Primary task two

Primary task three

Secondary tasks

- [ ]
- [ ]
- [ ]
- [ ]
- [ ]

If you could live this day again, what would you do differently this time?

-
-
-

What am I grateful for today?

-
-
-
-

Appointments

	:
	:
	:
	:
	:
	:
	:
	:
	:
	:
	:
	:
	:
	:

Hero on a Mission Daily Planner

Date

My Morning Ritual

- [ ] I've read my eulogy
- [ ] I've reviewed my vision worksheets
- [ ] I've reviewed my goals

Primary task one

Primary task two

Primary task three

Secondary tasks

- [ ]
- [ ]
- [ ]
- [ ]
- [ ]

If you could live this day again, what would you do differently this time?

-
-
-

What am I grateful for today?

-
-
-
-

Appointments

Hero on a Mission Daily Planner

Date

My Morning Ritual

- [ ] I've read my eulogy
- [ ] I've reviewed my vision worksheets
- [ ] I've reviewed my goals

Primary task one

Primary task two

Primary task three

Secondary tasks

If you could live this day again, what would you do differently this time?

What am I grateful for today?

Appointments

Hero on a Mission Daily Planner

Date

My Morning Ritual

- [ ] I've read my eulogy
- [ ] I've reviewed my vision worksheets
- [ ] I've reviewed my goals

Primary task one

Primary task two

Primary task three

Secondary tasks

- [ ]
- [ ]
- [ ]
- [ ]
- [ ]

If you could live this day again, what would you do differently this time?

-
-
-

What am I grateful for today?

-
-
-
-

Appointments

Hero on a Mission Daily Planner

Date

My Morning Ritual

- [ ] I've read my eulogy
- [ ] I've reviewed my vision worksheets
- [ ] I've reviewed my goals

Primary task one

Primary task two

Primary task three

Secondary tasks

- [ ]
- [ ]
- [ ]
- [ ]
- [ ]

If you could live this day again, what would you do differently this time?

What am I grateful for today?

Appointments

"To me, meaning does not feel like joy or even pleasure. I've had plenty of bad days in the midst of experiencing meaning. Meaning is better than that. Meaning feels like purpose."

From *Hero on a Mission*

MANKIND DOES NOT exist to pursue pleasure. Mankind exists to pursue meaning, and people distract themselves with pleasure when they can't find meaning.

Hero on a Mission Daily Planner

Date

My Morning Ritual

- [ ] I've read my eulogy
- [ ] I've reviewed my vision worksheets
- [ ] I've reviewed my goals

Primary task one

Primary task two

Primary task three

Secondary tasks

- [ ]
- [ ]
- [ ]
- [ ]
- [ ]

If you could live this day again, what would you do differently this time?

-
-
-

What am I grateful for today?

-
-
-
-

Appointments

	:
	:
	:
	:
	:
	:
	:
	:
	:
	:
	:
	:
	:

Hero on a Mission Daily Planner

Date

My Morning Ritual

☐ I've read my eulogy

☐ I've reviewed my vision worksheets

☐ I've reviewed my goals

Primary task one

Primary task two

Primary task three

Secondary tasks

☐
☐
☐
☐
☐

If you could live this day again, what would you do differently this time?

•
•
•

What am I grateful for today?

•
•
•
•

Appointments

Hero on a Mission Daily Planner

Date

My Morning Ritual

- ☐ I've read my eulogy
- ☐ I've reviewed my vision worksheets
- ☐ I've reviewed my goals

Primary task one

Primary task two

Primary task three

Secondary tasks

- ☐
- ☐
- ☐
- ☐
- ☐

If you could live this day again, what would you do differently this time?

-
-
-

What am I grateful for today?

-
-
-
-

Appointments

:
:
:
:
:
:
:
:
:
:
:
:
:

Hero on a Mission Daily Planner

Date

My Morning Ritual

- [ ] I've read my eulogy
- [ ] I've reviewed my vision worksheets
- [ ] I've reviewed my goals

Primary task one

Primary task two

Primary task three

Secondary tasks

- [ ]
- [ ]
- [ ]
- [ ]
- [ ]

If you could live this day again, what would you do differently this time?

-
-
-

What am I grateful for today?

-
-
-
-

Appointments

Hero on a Mission Daily Planner

Date

My Morning Ritual

- [ ] I've read my eulogy
- [ ] I've reviewed my vision worksheets
- [ ] I've reviewed my goals

Primary task one

Primary task two

Primary task three

Secondary tasks

- [ ]
- [ ]
- [ ]
- [ ]
- [ ]

If you could live this day again, what would you do differently this time?

-
-
-

What am I grateful for today?

-
-
-
-

Appointments

	:
	:
	:
	:
	:
	:
	:
	:
	:
	:
	:
	:
	:
	:

Hero on a Mission Daily Planner

Date

My Morning Ritual

- [ ] I've read my eulogy
- [ ] I've reviewed my vision worksheets
- [ ] I've reviewed my goals

Primary task one

Primary task two

Primary task three

Secondary tasks

- [ ]
- [ ]
- [ ]
- [ ]
- [ ]

If you could live this day again, what would you do differently this time?

-
-
-

What am I grateful for today?

-
-
-
-

Appointments

Hero on a Mission Daily Planner

Date

My Morning Ritual

- [ ] I've read my eulogy
- [ ] I've reviewed my vision worksheets
- [ ] I've reviewed my goals

Primary task one

Primary task two

Primary task three

Secondary tasks

If you could live this day again, what would you do differently this time?

What am I grateful for today?

Appointments

"It's my belief that meaning is philosophically and theologically agnostic. You can be an atheist, a Christian, a Muslim, or anything and experience meaning, just as you can be an atheist, a Christian, or a Muslim and experience joy and love."

From *Hero on a Mission*

GOD IS GENEROUS with the feeling of meaning. God gives meaning to any person who takes action toward something difficult and good. God is not stingy with the feelings of wonder, joy, love, and meaning.

Hero on a Mission Daily Planner

Date

My Morning Ritual

- [ ] I've read my eulogy
- [ ] I've reviewed my vision worksheets
- [ ] I've reviewed my goals

Primary task one

Primary task two

Primary task three

Secondary tasks

If you could live this day again, what would you do differently this time?

What am I grateful for today?

Appointments

Hero on a Mission Daily Planner

Date

My Morning Ritual

- [ ] I've read my eulogy
- [ ] I've reviewed my vision worksheets
- [ ] I've reviewed my goals

Primary task one

Primary task two

Primary task three

Secondary tasks

- [ ]
- [ ]
- [ ]
- [ ]
- [ ]

If you could live this day again, what would you do differently this time?

-
-
-

What am I grateful for today?

-
-
-
-

Appointments

Hero on a Mission Daily Planner

Date

My Morning Ritual

- [ ] I've read my eulogy
- [ ] I've reviewed my vision worksheets
- [ ] I've reviewed my goals

Primary task one

Primary task two

Primary task three

Secondary tasks

- [ ]
- [ ]
- [ ]
- [ ]
- [ ]

If you could live this day again, what would you do differently this time?

-
-
-

What am I grateful for today?

-
-
-
-

Appointments

Hero on a Mission Daily Planner

Date

My Morning Ritual

- [ ] I've read my eulogy
- [ ] I've reviewed my vision worksheets
- [ ] I've reviewed my goals

Primary task one

Primary task two

Primary task three

Secondary tasks

- [ ]
- [ ]
- [ ]
- [ ]
- [ ]

If you could live this day again, what would you do differently this time?

-
-
-

What am I grateful for today?

-
-
-
-

Appointments

	:
	:
	:
	:
	:
	:
	:
	:
	:
	:
	:
	:
	:

Hero on a Mission Daily Planner

Date

My Morning Ritual

- [ ] I've read my eulogy
- [ ] I've reviewed my vision worksheets
- [ ] I've reviewed my goals

Primary task one

Primary task two

Primary task three

Secondary tasks

- [ ]
- [ ]
- [ ]
- [ ]
- [ ]

If you could live this day again, what would you do differently this time?

-
-
-

What am I grateful for today?

-
-
-
-

Appointments

	:
	:
	:
	:
	:
	:
	:
	:
	:
	:
	:
	:
	:
	:

Hero on a Mission Daily Planner

Date

My Morning Ritual

- [ ] I've read my eulogy
- [ ] I've reviewed my vision worksheets
- [ ] I've reviewed my goals

Primary task one

Primary task two

Primary task three

Secondary tasks

- [ ]
- [ ]
- [ ]
- [ ]
- [ ]

If you could live this day again, what would you do differently this time?

-
-
-

What am I grateful for today?

-
-
-
-

Appointments

Hero on a Mission Daily Planner

Date

My Morning Ritual

- [ ] I've read my eulogy
- [ ] I've reviewed my vision worksheets
- [ ] I've reviewed my goals

Primary task one

Primary task two

Primary task three

Secondary tasks

- [ ]
- [ ]
- [ ]
- [ ]
- [ ]

If you could live this day again, what would you do differently this time?

-
-
-

What am I grateful for today?

-
-
-
-

Appointments

"Intuitively, we all know that pain is the force that transforms us."

From *Hero on a Mission*

NONE OF US wants to experience pain, but pain does have a philosophical (and narrative) bright side. It transforms us. If you could delete the most painful season from your memory, would you do it? Most people say no. They intuitively know that while the experience was excruciating, it also made them stronger, more empathetic, more kind, and more resilient. Somehow, in the pain, there was meaning and transformation.

Hero on a Mission Daily Planner

Date

My Morning Ritual

- [ ] I've read my eulogy
- [ ] I've reviewed my vision worksheets
- [ ] I've reviewed my goals

Primary task one

Primary task two

Primary task three

Secondary tasks

If you could live this day again, what would you do differently this time?

What am I grateful for today?

Appointments

Hero on a Mission Daily Planner

Date

My Morning Ritual

- [ ] I've read my eulogy
- [ ] I've reviewed my vision worksheets
- [ ] I've reviewed my goals

Primary task one

Primary task two

Primary task three

Secondary tasks

- [ ]
- [ ]
- [ ]
- [ ]
- [ ]

If you could live this day again, what would you do differently this time?

-
-
-

What am I grateful for today?

-
-
-
-

Appointments

	:
	:
	:
	:
	:
	:
	:
	:
	:
	:
	:
	:
	:
	:

Hero on a Mission Daily Planner

Date

My Morning Ritual

- [ ] I've read my eulogy
- [ ] I've reviewed my vision worksheets
- [ ] I've reviewed my goals

Primary task one

Primary task two

Primary task three

Secondary tasks

If you could live this day again, what would you do differently this time?

What am I grateful for today?

Appointments

Hero on a Mission Daily Planner

Date

My Morning Ritual

- [ ] I've read my eulogy
- [ ] I've reviewed my vision worksheets
- [ ] I've reviewed my goals

Primary task one

Primary task two

Primary task three

Secondary tasks

- [ ]
- [ ]
- [ ]
- [ ]
- [ ]

If you could live this day again, what would you do differently this time?

-
-
-

What am I grateful for today?

-
-
-
-

Appointments

Hero on a Mission Daily Planner

Date

My Morning Ritual

- ☐ I've read my eulogy
- ☐ I've reviewed my vision worksheets
- ☐ I've reviewed my goals

Primary task one

Primary task two

Primary task three

Secondary tasks

- ☐
- ☐
- ☐
- ☐
- ☐

If you could live this day again, what would you do differently this time?

-
-
-

What am I grateful for today?

-
-
-
-

Appointments

"The general rule is that a hero does not have to be perfect; they just have to consistently transform into a better version of themselves."

From *Hero on a Mission*

HEROES AREN'T PERFECT. They are usually afraid, unwilling to take action, ill equipped for the challenge before them, and in desperate need of help. It's the journey that turns them into a hero. The challenge transforms them into a better version of themselves.

Hero on a Mission Daily Planner

Date

My Morning Ritual

- [ ] I've read my eulogy
- [ ] I've reviewed my vision worksheets
- [ ] I've reviewed my goals

Primary task one

Primary task two

Primary task three

Secondary tasks

- [ ]
- [ ]
- [ ]
- [ ]
- [ ]

If you could live this day again, what would you do differently this time?

-
-
-

What am I grateful for today?

-
-
-
-

Appointments

Hero on a Mission Daily Planner

Date

My Morning Ritual

- [ ] I've read my eulogy
- [ ] I've reviewed my vision worksheets
- [ ] I've reviewed my goals

Primary task one

Primary task two

Primary task three

Secondary tasks

- [ ]
- [ ]
- [ ]
- [ ]
- [ ]

If you could live this day again, what would you do differently this time?

-
-
-

What am I grateful for today?

-
-
-
-

Appointments

Hero on a Mission Daily Planner

Date

My Morning Ritual

- [ ] I've read my eulogy
- [ ] I've reviewed my vision worksheets
- [ ] I've reviewed my goals

Primary task one

Primary task two

Primary task three

Secondary tasks

- [ ]
- [ ]
- [ ]
- [ ]
- [ ]

If you could live this day again, what would you do differently this time?

-
-
-

What am I grateful for today?

-
-
-
-

Appointments

	:
	:
	:
	:
	:
	:
	:
	:
	:
	:
	:
	:
	:
	:

Hero on a Mission Daily Planner

Date

My Morning Ritual

- [ ] I've read my eulogy
- [ ] I've reviewed my vision worksheets
- [ ] I've reviewed my goals

Primary task one

Primary task two

Primary task three

Secondary tasks

- [ ]
- [ ]
- [ ]
- [ ]
- [ ]

If you could live this day again, what would you do differently this time?

-
-
-

What am I grateful for today?

-
-
-
-

Appointments

Hero on a Mission Daily Planner

Date

My Morning Ritual

- [ ] I've read my eulogy
- [ ] I've reviewed my vision worksheets
- [ ] I've reviewed my goals

Primary task one

Primary task two

Primary task three

Secondary tasks

- [ ]
- [ ]
- [ ]
- [ ]
- [ ]

If you could live this day again, what would you do differently this time?

What am I grateful for today?

Appointments

Hero on a Mission Daily Planner

Date

My Morning Ritual

- [ ] I've read my eulogy
- [ ] I've reviewed my vision worksheets
- [ ] I've reviewed my goals

Primary task one

Primary task two

Primary task three

Secondary tasks

- [ ]
- [ ]
- [ ]
- [ ]
- [ ]

If you could live this day again, what would you do differently this time?

-
-
-

What am I grateful for today?

-
-
-
-

Appointments

Hero on a Mission Daily Planner

Date

My Morning Ritual

- [ ] I've read my eulogy
- [ ] I've reviewed my vision worksheets
- [ ] I've reviewed my goals

Primary task one

Primary task two

Primary task three

Secondary tasks

- [ ]
- [ ]
- [ ]
- [ ]
- [ ]

If you could live this day again, what would you do differently this time?

What am I grateful for today?

Appointments

"Midlife crisis happens when the cultural scripts end but we fail to write a new story for ourselves."

From *Hero on a Mission*

OUR PARENTS INVITE us into a story about learning life, then our schools and colleges invite us to get degrees and start a story about our careers, culture invites us to get married and have children, and our careers invite us to succeed. Then, at about forty, culture stops handing us scripts. Some people don't know what to do. They sit in the theater of their mind watching a blank screen, feeling that the story they are living is meaningless. What they never realized is that it was their turn to write a story for themselves. Culture was never responsible for their lives; they were responsible for their lives. Those who create a new story for themselves experience a deep sense of meaning, and those who do not may experience a midlife crisis.

Hero on a Mission Daily Planner

Date

My Morning Ritual

- [ ] I've read my eulogy
- [ ] I've reviewed my vision worksheets
- [ ] I've reviewed my goals

Primary task one

Primary task two

Primary task three

Secondary tasks

- [ ]
- [ ]
- [ ]
- [ ]
- [ ]

If you could live this day again, what would you do differently this time?

-
-
-

What am I grateful for today?

-
-
-
-

Appointments

:
:
:
:
:
:
:
:
:
:
:
:
:

Hero on a Mission Daily Planner

Date

My Morning Ritual

- [ ] I've read my eulogy
- [ ] I've reviewed my vision worksheets
- [ ] I've reviewed my goals

Primary task one

Primary task two

Primary task three

Secondary tasks

- [ ]
- [ ]
- [ ]
- [ ]
- [ ]

If you could live this day again, what would you do differently this time?

-
-
-

What am I grateful for today?

-
-
-
-

Appointments

	:
	:
	:
	:
	:
	:
	:
	:
	:
	:
	:
	:
	:

Hero on a Mission Daily Planner

Date

My Morning Ritual

- [ ] I've read my eulogy
- [ ] I've reviewed my vision worksheets
- [ ] I've reviewed my goals

Primary task one

Primary task two

Primary task three

Secondary tasks

- [ ]
- [ ]
- [ ]
- [ ]
- [ ]

If you could live this day again, what would you do differently this time?

What am I grateful for today?

Appointments

Hero on a Mission Daily Planner

Date

My Morning Ritual

- [ ] I've read my eulogy
- [ ] I've reviewed my vision worksheets
- [ ] I've reviewed my goals

Primary task one

Primary task two

Primary task three

Secondary tasks

- [ ]
- [ ]
- [ ]
- [ ]
- [ ]

If you could live this day again, what would you do differently this time?

-
-
-

What am I grateful for today?

-
-
-
-

Appointments

Hero on a Mission Daily Planner

Date

My Morning Ritual

- [ ] I've read my eulogy
- [ ] I've reviewed my vision worksheets
- [ ] I've reviewed my goals

Primary task one

Primary task two

Primary task three

Secondary tasks

- [ ]
- [ ]
- [ ]
- [ ]
- [ ]

If you could live this day again, what would you do differently this time?

-
-
-

What am I grateful for today?

-
-
-
-

Appointments

Hero on a Mission Daily Planner

Date

My Morning Ritual

- [ ] I've read my eulogy
- [ ] I've reviewed my vision worksheets
- [ ] I've reviewed my goals

Primary task one

Primary task two

Primary task three

Secondary tasks

- [ ]
- [ ]
- [ ]
- [ ]
- [ ]

If you could live this day again, what would you do differently this time?

-
-
-

What am I grateful for today?

-
-
-
-

Appointments

Hero on a Mission Daily Planner

Date

My Morning Ritual

- [ ] I've read my eulogy
- [ ] I've reviewed my vision worksheets
- [ ] I've reviewed my goals

Primary task one

Primary task two

Primary task three

Secondary tasks

If you could live this day again, what would you do differently this time?

What am I grateful for today?

Appointments

"Growing up, I used to sing along with Bono as he cried out that he still hadn't found what he was looking for. I still sing along with Bono, but it feels different now. I still haven't found what I'm looking for either, but having discovered a deep sense of meaning I am now uninterested in the search for anything else. I am fulfilled, even in the unknowing. I do not want to live life looking for something I don't have. I want to become more and more interested in the opportunities I've been given. In short, I am pleasantly distracted by meaning."

From *Hero on a Mission*

MEANING DOESN'T FULFILL our deepest longings—those longings that are a common part of the human experience. Meaning does, however, serve as a pleasant distraction. Meaning is experienced in motion. Even Jesus said "follow Me" rather than "figure Me out." We've spent way too much time studying meaning and way too little time experiencing meaning. Meaning happens when we move.

Hero on a Mission Daily Planner

Date

My Morning Ritual

- [ ] I've read my eulogy
- [ ] I've reviewed my vision worksheets
- [ ] I've reviewed my goals

Primary task one

Primary task two

Primary task three

Secondary tasks

- [ ]
- [ ]
- [ ]
- [ ]
- [ ]

If you could live this day again, what would you do differently this time?

-
-
-

What am I grateful for today?

-
-
-
-

Appointments

:
:
:
:
:
:
:
:
:
:
:
:
:

Hero on a Mission Daily Planner

Date

My Morning Ritual

- [ ] I've read my eulogy
- [ ] I've reviewed my vision worksheets
- [ ] I've reviewed my goals

Primary task one

Primary task two

Primary task three

Secondary tasks

- [ ]
- [ ]
- [ ]
- [ ]
- [ ]

If you could live this day again, what would you do differently this time?

-
-
-

What am I grateful for today?

-
-
-
-

Appointments

Hero on a Mission Daily Planner

Date

My Morning Ritual

- [ ] I've read my eulogy
- [ ] I've reviewed my vision worksheets
- [ ] I've reviewed my goals

Primary task one

Primary task two

Primary task three

Secondary tasks

- [ ]
- [ ]
- [ ]
- [ ]
- [ ]

If you could live this day again, what would you do differently this time?

-
-
-

What am I grateful for today?

-
-
-
-

Appointments

Hero on a Mission Daily Planner

Date

My Morning Ritual

- [ ] I've read my eulogy
- [ ] I've reviewed my vision worksheets
- [ ] I've reviewed my goals

Primary task one

Primary task two

Primary task three

Secondary tasks

- [ ]
- [ ]
- [ ]
- [ ]
- [ ]

If you could live this day again, what would you do differently this time?

-
-
-

What am I grateful for today?

-
-
-
-

Appointments

Hero on a Mission Daily Planner

Date

My Morning Ritual

- ☐ I've read my eulogy
- ☐ I've reviewed my vision worksheets
- ☐ I've reviewed my goals

Primary task one

Primary task two

Primary task three

Secondary tasks

- ☐
- ☐
- ☐
- ☐
- ☐

If you could live this day again, what would you do differently this time?

-
-
-

What am I grateful for today?

-
-
-
-

Appointments

Hero on a Mission Daily Planner

Date

My Morning Ritual

- [ ] I've read my eulogy
- [ ] I've reviewed my vision worksheets
- [ ] I've reviewed my goals

Primary task one

Primary task two

Primary task three

Secondary tasks

- [ ]
- [ ]
- [ ]
- [ ]
- [ ]

If you could live this day again, what would you do differently this time?

-
-
-

What am I grateful for today?

-
-
-
-

Appointments

Hero on a Mission Daily Planner

Date

My Morning Ritual

- [ ] I've read my eulogy
- [ ] I've reviewed my vision worksheets
- [ ] I've reviewed my goals

Primary task one

Primary task two

Primary task three

Secondary tasks

- [ ]
- [ ]
- [ ]
- [ ]
- [ ]

If you could live this day again, what would you do differently this time?

-
-
-

What am I grateful for today?

-
-
-
-

Appointments

"People who are not honest about their nuanced motives are driven by the most deceptive desire of all: they want to believe they are perfect. In truth, they want to believe they are better than you. And there is nothing selfless about that."

From *Hero on a Mission*

THERE WERE MANY wonderful things about growing up in an evangelical church, including a strong sense of community and an appropriate honoring of morality. The downside is that when a culture upholds a moral order, some feel they have to fake it to fit in. Many, in order to rise in prominence inside an evangelical culture, will become public opposites of their true selves. This, of course, is deception. It is ironic, then, that in their attempt to uphold godliness, they become a conspirator with the father of lies. The truth is people are nuanced. They aren't perfect, and they don't have to be in order to live a heroic story. Beware of those who act perfect. People who act perfect are secretly arrogant and self-absorbed.

Hero on a Mission Daily Planner

Date

My Morning Ritual

- ☐ I've read my eulogy
- ☐ I've reviewed my vision worksheets
- ☐ I've reviewed my goals

Primary task one

Primary task two

Primary task three

Secondary tasks

- ☐
- ☐
- ☐
- ☐
- ☐

If you could live this day again, what would you do differently this time?

-
-
-

What am I grateful for today?

-
-
-
-

Appointments

	:
	:
	:
	:
	:
	:
	:
	:
	:
	:
	:
	:
	:

Hero on a Mission Daily Planner

Date

My Morning Ritual

- [ ] I've read my eulogy
- [ ] I've reviewed my vision worksheets
- [ ] I've reviewed my goals

Primary task one

Primary task two

Primary task three

Secondary tasks

- [ ]
- [ ]
- [ ]
- [ ]
- [ ]

If you could live this day again, what would you do differently this time?

-
-
-

What am I grateful for today?

-
-
-
-

Appointments

Hero on a Mission Daily Planner

Date

My Morning Ritual

- [ ] I've read my eulogy
- [ ] I've reviewed my vision worksheets
- [ ] I've reviewed my goals

Primary task one

Primary task two

Primary task three

Secondary tasks

- [ ]
- [ ]
- [ ]
- [ ]
- [ ]

If you could live this day again, what would you do differently this time?

-
-
-

What am I grateful for today?

-
-
-
-

Appointments

Hero on a Mission Daily Planner

Date

My Morning Ritual

- [ ] I've read my eulogy
- [ ] I've reviewed my vision worksheets
- [ ] I've reviewed my goals

Primary task one

Primary task two

Primary task three

Secondary tasks

- [ ]
- [ ]
- [ ]
- [ ]
- [ ]

If you could live this day again, what would you do differently this time?

-
-
-

What am I grateful for today?

-
-
-
-

Appointments

Hero on a Mission Daily Planner

Date

My Morning Ritual

☐ I've read my eulogy

☐ I've reviewed my vision worksheets

☐ I've reviewed my goals

Primary task one

Primary task two

Primary task three

Secondary tasks

☐
☐
☐
☐
☐

If you could live this day again, what would you do differently this time?

-
-
-

What am I grateful for today?

-
-
-
-

Appendix

Appointments

:
:
:
:
:
:
:
:
:
:
:
:
:

"A storyteller has to make choices. In life, heroes on a mission also have to make choices. After filmmakers edit a movie, there are often as many scenes on the cutting-room floor as there are in the film itself. An editor knows that an audience cannot follow a story that isn't clean."

From *Hero on a Mission*

WHEN WE TRY to do everything, we accomplish little. Every good storyteller makes decisions. Most of those decisions involve leaving stuff out.

Hero on a Mission Daily Planner

Date

My Morning Ritual

- [ ] I've read my eulogy
- [ ] I've reviewed my vision worksheets
- [ ] I've reviewed my goals

Primary task one

Primary task two

Primary task three

Secondary tasks

- [ ]
- [ ]
- [ ]
- [ ]
- [ ]

If you could live this day again, what would you do differently this time?

-
-
-

What am I grateful for today?

-
-
-
-

Appointments

:
:
:
:
:
:
:
:
:
:
:
:
:

Hero on a Mission Daily Planner

Date

My Morning Ritual

- ☐ I've read my eulogy
- ☐ I've reviewed my vision worksheets
- ☐ I've reviewed my goals

Primary task one

Primary task two

Primary task three

Secondary tasks

- ☐
- ☐
- ☐
- ☐
- ☐

If you could live this day again, what would you do differently this time?

-
-
-

What am I grateful for today?

-
-
-
-

Appointments

	:
	:
	:
	:
	:
	:
	:
	:
	:
	:
	:
	:
	:

Hero on a Mission Daily Planner

Date

My Morning Ritual

- ☐ I've read my eulogy
- ☐ I've reviewed my vision worksheets
- ☐ I've reviewed my goals

Primary task one

Primary task two

Primary task three

Secondary tasks

- ☐
- ☐
- ☐
- ☐
- ☐

If you could live this day again, what would you do differently this time?

-
-
-

What am I grateful for today?

-
-
-
-

Appointments

Hero on a Mission Daily Planner

Date

My Morning Ritual

- ☐ I've read my eulogy
- ☐ I've reviewed my vision worksheets
- ☐ I've reviewed my goals

Primary task one

Primary task two

Primary task three

Secondary tasks

- ☐
- ☐
- ☐
- ☐
- ☐

If you could live this day again, what would you do differently this time?

-
-
-

What am I grateful for today?

-
-
-
-

Appointments

Hero on a Mission Daily Planner

Date

My Morning Ritual

- [ ] I've read my eulogy
- [ ] I've reviewed my vision worksheets
- [ ] I've reviewed my goals

Primary task one

Primary task two

Primary task three

Secondary tasks

If you could live this day again, what would you do differently this time?

What am I grateful for today?

Appointments

Hero on a Mission Daily Planner

Date

My Morning Ritual

- [ ] I've read my eulogy
- [ ] I've reviewed my vision worksheets
- [ ] I've reviewed my goals

Primary task one

Primary task two

Primary task three

Secondary tasks

- [ ]
- [ ]
- [ ]
- [ ]
- [ ]

If you could live this day again, what would you do differently this time?

-
-
-

What am I grateful for today?

-
-
-
-

Appointments

Hero on a Mission Daily Planner

Date

My Morning Ritual

- [ ] I've read my eulogy
- [ ] I've reviewed my vision worksheets
- [ ] I've reviewed my goals

Primary task one

Primary task two

Primary task three

Secondary tasks

- [ ]
- [ ]
- [ ]
- [ ]
- [ ]

If you could live this day again, what would you do differently this time?

What am I grateful for today?

Appointments

"Find the story you want to live and you won't have to worry about discipline."

From *Hero on a Mission*

I DON'T GET up early every morning to write because I'm disciplined. I get up early to write because I love to write. I love being a writer. This is one of the great deceptions of Instagram: supposedly disciplined people shaming undisciplined people. The truth is, those who love their own story don't need discipline. It's a lot easier to make sacrifices when you are fully interested in your own narrative. Success isn't about discipline; it's about finding a challenge you love so much you don't need discipline. Replace discipline with desire and you'll be fine.

Hero on a Mission Daily Planner

Date

My Morning Ritual

- [ ] I've read my eulogy
- [ ] I've reviewed my vision worksheets
- [ ] I've reviewed my goals

Primary task one

Primary task two

Primary task three

Secondary tasks

- [ ]
- [ ]
- [ ]
- [ ]
- [ ]

If you could live this day again, what would you do differently this time?

-
-
-

What am I grateful for today?

-
-
-
-

Appointments

Hero on a Mission Daily Planner

Date

My Morning Ritual

- ☐ I've read my eulogy
- ☐ I've reviewed my vision worksheets
- ☐ I've reviewed my goals

Primary task one

Primary task two

Primary task three

Secondary tasks

- ☐
- ☐
- ☐
- ☐
- ☐

If you could live this day again, what would you do differently this time?

-
-
-

What am I grateful for today?

-
-
-
-

Appointments

:
:
:
:
:
:
:
:
:
:
:
:
:

Hero on a Mission Daily Planner

Date

My Morning Ritual

- [ ] I've read my eulogy
- [ ] I've reviewed my vision worksheets
- [ ] I've reviewed my goals

Primary task one

Primary task two

Primary task three

Secondary tasks

- [ ]
- [ ]
- [ ]
- [ ]
- [ ]

If you could live this day again, what would you do differently this time?

-
-
-

What am I grateful for today?

-
-
-
-

Appointments

	:
	:
	:
	:
	:
	:
	:
	:
	:
	:
	:
	:
	:
	:

Hero on a Mission Daily Planner

Date

My Morning Ritual

- ☐ I've read my eulogy
- ☐ I've reviewed my vision worksheets
- ☐ I've reviewed my goals

Primary task one

Primary task two

Primary task three

Secondary tasks

- ☐
- ☐
- ☐
- ☐
- ☐

If you could live this day again, what would you do differently this time?

-
-
-

What am I grateful for today?

-
-
-
-

Appointments

Hero on a Mission Daily Planner

Date

My Morning Ritual

- [ ] I've read my eulogy
- [ ] I've reviewed my vision worksheets
- [ ] I've reviewed my goals

Primary task one

Primary task two

Primary task three

Secondary tasks

- [ ]
- [ ]
- [ ]
- [ ]
- [ ]

If you could live this day again, what would you do differently this time?

-
-
-

What am I grateful for today?

-
-
-
-

Appointments

"When our babies cry in the night and we are tired and dragging and wonder if we have lost our freedom, the answer is yes. We have lost our freedom. But we have gained meaning."

From *Hero on a Mission*

SOME OF THE most difficult seasons of our lives will be remembered with a sentimental fondness. It's the sacrifice that builds meaning into our memories.

Hero on a Mission Daily Planner

Date

My Morning Ritual

- [ ] I've read my eulogy
- [ ] I've reviewed my vision worksheets
- [ ] I've reviewed my goals

Primary task one

Primary task two

Primary task three

Secondary tasks

- [ ]
- [ ]
- [ ]
- [ ]
- [ ]

If you could live this day again, what would you do differently this time?

What am I grateful for today?

Appointments

Hero on a Mission Daily Planner

Date

My Morning Ritual

- [ ] I've read my eulogy
- [ ] I've reviewed my vision worksheets
- [ ] I've reviewed my goals

Primary task one

Primary task two

Primary task three

Secondary tasks

- [ ]
- [ ]
- [ ]
- [ ]
- [ ]

If you could live this day again, what would you do differently this time?

-
-
-

What am I grateful for today?

-
-
-
-

Appointments

	:
	:
	:
	:
	:
	:
	:
	:
	:
	:
	:
	:
	:

Hero on a Mission Daily Planner

Date

My Morning Ritual

- [ ] I've read my eulogy
- [ ] I've reviewed my vision worksheets
- [ ] I've reviewed my goals

Primary task one

Primary task two

Primary task three

Secondary tasks

- [ ]
- [ ]
- [ ]
- [ ]
- [ ]

If you could live this day again, what would you do differently this time?

-
-
-

What am I grateful for today?

-
-
-
-

Appointments

	:
	:
	:
	:
	:
	:
	:
	:
	:
	:
	:
	:
	:

Hero on a Mission Daily Planner

Date

My Morning Ritual

- [ ] I've read my eulogy
- [ ] I've reviewed my vision worksheets
- [ ] I've reviewed my goals

Primary task one

Primary task two

Primary task three

Secondary tasks

- [ ]
- [ ]
- [ ]
- [ ]
- [ ]

If you could live this day again, what would you do differently this time?

-
-
-

What am I grateful for today?

-
-
-
-

Appointments

Hero on a Mission Daily Planner

Date

My Morning Ritual

- [ ] I've read my eulogy
- [ ] I've reviewed my vision worksheets
- [ ] I've reviewed my goals

Primary task one

Primary task two

Primary task three

Secondary tasks

- [ ]
- [ ]
- [ ]
- [ ]
- [ ]

If you could live this day again, what would you do differently this time?

-
-
-

What am I grateful for today?

-
-
-
-

Appointments

Hero on a Mission Daily Planner

Date

My Morning Ritual

- ☐ I've read my eulogy
- ☐ I've reviewed my vision worksheets
- ☐ I've reviewed my goals

Primary task one

Primary task two

Primary task three

Secondary tasks

- ☐
- ☐
- ☐
- ☐
- ☐

If you could live this day again, what would you do differently this time?

-
-
-

What am I grateful for today?

-
-
-
-

Appointments

	:
	:
	:
	:
	:
	:
	:
	:
	:
	:
	:
	:
	:

Hero on a Mission Daily Planner

Date

My Morning Ritual

- ☐ I've read my eulogy
- ☐ I've reviewed my vision worksheets
- ☐ I've reviewed my goals

Primary task one

Primary task two

Primary task three

Secondary tasks

- ☐
- ☐
- ☐
- ☐
- ☐

If you could live this day again, what would you do differently this time?

-
-
-

What am I grateful for today?

-
-
-
-

Appointments

	:
	:
	:
	:
	:
	:
	:
	:
	:
	:
	:
	:
	:
	:

"Stories may be told through the lens of the hero, but they are almost always about what is happening to a community of people."

From *Hero on a Mission*

IT'S THE PEOPLE around us that fill our lives with meaning. Without them, our stories and our lives would feel empty.

Hero on a Mission Daily Planner

Date

My Morning Ritual

- ☐ I've read my eulogy
- ☐ I've reviewed my vision worksheets
- ☐ I've reviewed my goals

Primary task one

Primary task two

Primary task three

Secondary tasks

- ☐
- ☐
- ☐
- ☐
- ☐

If you could live this day again, what would you do differently this time?

-
-
-

What am I grateful for today?

-
-
-
-

Appointments

Hero on a Mission Daily Planner

Date

My Morning Ritual

- [ ] I've read my eulogy
- [ ] I've reviewed my vision worksheets
- [ ] I've reviewed my goals

Primary task one

Primary task two

Primary task three

Secondary tasks

- [ ]
- [ ]
- [ ]
- [ ]
- [ ]

If you could live this day again, what would you do differently this time?

-
-
-

What am I grateful for today?

-
-
-
-

Appointments

Hero on a Mission Daily Planner

Date

My Morning Ritual

- [ ] I've read my eulogy
- [ ] I've reviewed my vision worksheets
- [ ] I've reviewed my goals

Primary task one

Primary task two

Primary task three

Secondary tasks

- [ ]
- [ ]
- [ ]
- [ ]
- [ ]

If you could live this day again, what would you do differently this time?

-
-
-

What am I grateful for today?

-
-
-
-

Appointments

Hero on a Mission Daily Planner

Date

My Morning Ritual

- [ ] I've read my eulogy
- [ ] I've reviewed my vision worksheets
- [ ] I've reviewed my goals

Primary task one

Primary task two

Primary task three

Secondary tasks

- [ ]
- [ ]
- [ ]
- [ ]
- [ ]

If you could live this day again, what would you do differently this time?

-
-
-

What am I grateful for today?

-
-
-
-

Appointments

Hero on a Mission Daily Planner

Date

My Morning Ritual

- [ ] I've read my eulogy
- [ ] I've reviewed my vision worksheets
- [ ] I've reviewed my goals

Primary task one

Primary task two

Primary task three

Secondary tasks

- [ ]
- [ ]
- [ ]
- [ ]
- [ ]

If you could live this day again, what would you do differently this time?

-
-
-

What am I grateful for today?

-
-
-
-

Appointments

Hero on a Mission Daily Planner

Date

My Morning Ritual

- [ ] I've read my eulogy
- [ ] I've reviewed my vision worksheets
- [ ] I've reviewed my goals

Primary task one

Primary task two

Primary task three

Secondary tasks

- [ ]
- [ ]
- [ ]
- [ ]
- [ ]

If you could live this day again, what would you do differently this time?

-
-
-

What am I grateful for today?

-
-
-
-

Appointments

	:
	:
	:
	:
	:
	:
	:
	:
	:
	:
	:
	:
	:

Hero on a Mission Daily Planner

Date

My Morning Ritual

- [ ] I've read my eulogy
- [ ] I've reviewed my vision worksheets
- [ ] I've reviewed my goals

Primary task one

Primary task two

Primary task three

Secondary tasks

- [ ]
- [ ]
- [ ]
- [ ]
- [ ]

If you could live this day again, what would you do differently this time?

-
-
-

What am I grateful for today?

-
-
-
-

Appointments

	:
	:
	:
	:
	:
	:
	:
	:
	:
	:
	:
	:
	:
	:

"The point is to start something or join something that creates narrative traction in our lives. Again, narrative traction is the feeling that our personal story is so interesting we can't turn away. We may not always like it, but we can't not do it. Even if it exhausts us and we find ourselves complaining about it, we're in it. The story has swallowed us up and is keeping us interested in our own lives."

From *Hero on a Mission*

IF OUR LIVES do not feel meaningful or interesting, we can change that by changing the dynamics of the story we are currently living. Want something that scares or embarrasses you. Want something that requires a challenge. Get up and put something on the plot every day. That's how we get narrative traction.

Hero on a Mission Daily Planner

Date

My Morning Ritual

- [ ] I've read my eulogy
- [ ] I've reviewed my vision worksheets
- [ ] I've reviewed my goals

Primary task one

Primary task two

Primary task three

Secondary tasks

- [ ]
- [ ]
- [ ]
- [ ]
- [ ]

If you could live this day again, what would you do differently this time?

-
-
-

What am I grateful for today?

-
-
-
-

Appointments

Hero on a Mission Daily Planner

Date

My Morning Ritual

- [ ] I've read my eulogy
- [ ] I've reviewed my vision worksheets
- [ ] I've reviewed my goals

Primary task one

Primary task two

Primary task three

Secondary tasks

- [ ]
- [ ]
- [ ]
- [ ]
- [ ]

If you could live this day again, what would you do differently this time?

-
-
-

What am I grateful for today?

-
-
-
-

Appointments

	:
	:
	:
	:
	:
	:
	:
	:
	:
	:
	:
	:
	:

Hero on a Mission Daily Planner

Date

My Morning Ritual

- [ ] I've read my eulogy
- [ ] I've reviewed my vision worksheets
- [ ] I've reviewed my goals

Primary task one

Primary task two

Primary task three

Secondary tasks

- [ ]
- [ ]
- [ ]
- [ ]
- [ ]

If you could live this day again, what would you do differently this time?

-
-
-

What am I grateful for today?

-
-
-
-

Appointments

Hero on a Mission Daily Planner

Date

My Morning Ritual

- [ ] I've read my eulogy
- [ ] I've reviewed my vision worksheets
- [ ] I've reviewed my goals

Primary task one

Primary task two

Primary task three

Secondary tasks

- [ ]
- [ ]
- [ ]
- [ ]
- [ ]

If you could live this day again, what would you do differently this time?

-
-
-

What am I grateful for today?

-
-
-
-

Appointments

Hero on a Mission Daily Planner

Date

My Morning Ritual

- [ ] I've read my eulogy
- [ ] I've reviewed my vision worksheets
- [ ] I've reviewed my goals

Primary task one

Primary task two

Primary task three

Secondary tasks

- [ ]
- [ ]
- [ ]
- [ ]
- [ ]

If you could live this day again, what would you do differently this time?

-
-
-

What am I grateful for today?

-
-
-
-

Appointments

	:
	:
	:
	:
	:
	:
	:
	:
	:
	:
	:
	:
	:

"I cling to the three things Ron Howard said he tried to provide for his children: love, security, and an example to follow."

From *Hero on a Mission*

MOST FATHERS FEEL like sous-chefs in the kitchen when it comes to raising kids. Mostly because Mom is infinitely more important in those early years. But fathers are critical. I was inspired by Ron Howard's three priorities and hope to live them out myself. Love. Security. An example to follow.

Hero on a Mission Daily Planner

Date

My Morning Ritual

- [ ] I've read my eulogy
- [ ] I've reviewed my vision worksheets
- [ ] I've reviewed my goals

Primary task one

Primary task two

Primary task three

Secondary tasks

- [ ]
- [ ]
- [ ]
- [ ]
- [ ]

If you could live this day again, what would you do differently this time?

-
-
-

What am I grateful for today?

-
-
-
-

Appointments

	:
	:
	:
	:
	:
	:
	:
	:
	:
	:
	:
	:
	:
	:

Hero on a Mission Daily Planner

Date

My Morning Ritual

- [ ] I've read my eulogy
- [ ] I've reviewed my vision worksheets
- [ ] I've reviewed my goals

Primary task one

Primary task two

Primary task three

Secondary tasks

- [ ]
- [ ]
- [ ]
- [ ]
- [ ]

If you could live this day again, what would you do differently this time?

-
-
-

What am I grateful for today?

-
-
-
-

Appointments

:
:
:
:
:
:
:
:
:
:
:
:
:

Hero on a Mission Daily Planner

Date

My Morning Ritual

- [ ] I've read my eulogy
- [ ] I've reviewed my vision worksheets
- [ ] I've reviewed my goals

Primary task one

Primary task two

Primary task three

Secondary tasks

- [ ]
- [ ]
- [ ]
- [ ]
- [ ]

If you could live this day again, what would you do differently this time?

-
-
-

What am I grateful for today?

-
-
-
-

Appointments

:
:
:
:
:
:
:
:
:
:
:
:
:

Hero on a Mission Daily Planner

Date

My Morning Ritual

- [ ] I've read my eulogy
- [ ] I've reviewed my vision worksheets
- [ ] I've reviewed my goals

Primary task one

Primary task two

Primary task three

Secondary tasks

- [ ]
- [ ]
- [ ]
- [ ]
- [ ]

If you could live this day again, what would you do differently this time?

-
-
-

What am I grateful for today?

-
-
-
-

Appointments

:

:

:

:

:

:

:

:

:

:

:

:

:

Hero on a Mission Daily Planner

Date

My Morning Ritual

- ☐ I've read my eulogy
- ☐ I've reviewed my vision worksheets
- ☐ I've reviewed my goals

Primary task one

Primary task two

Primary task three

Secondary tasks

- ☐
- ☐
- ☐
- ☐
- ☐

If you could live this day again, what would you do differently this time?

-
-
-

What am I grateful for today?

-
-
-
-

Appointments

Hero on a Mission Daily Planner

Date

My Morning Ritual

- [ ] I've read my eulogy
- [ ] I've reviewed my vision worksheets
- [ ] I've reviewed my goals

Primary task one

Primary task two

Primary task three

Secondary tasks

- [ ]
- [ ]
- [ ]
- [ ]
- [ ]

If you could live this day again, what would you do differently this time?

-
-
-

What am I grateful for today?

-
-
-
-

Appointments

Hero on a Mission Daily Planner

Date

My Morning Ritual

- [ ] I've read my eulogy
- [ ] I've reviewed my vision worksheets
- [ ] I've reviewed my goals

Primary task one

Primary task two

Primary task three

Secondary tasks

- [ ]
- [ ]
- [ ]
- [ ]
- [ ]

If you could live this day again, what would you do differently this time?

-
-
-

What am I grateful for today?

-
-
-
-

Appointments

	:
	:
	:
	:
	:
	:
	:
	:
	:
	:
	:
	:
	:
	:

“Villains do not have friends, they have minions. Villains surround themselves with people who do their bidding out of fear. To the villain, people are expendable. They do not love people; they use people.”

From *Hero on a Mission*

OUR VILLAINOUS SIDES want to use people. It’s an easy trap to step into. If our ambitions are causing us to use people rather than partner with them, our ambitions aren’t worth pursuing.

Hero on a Mission Daily Planner

Date

My Morning Ritual

- [ ] I've read my eulogy
- [ ] I've reviewed my vision worksheets
- [ ] I've reviewed my goals

Primary task one

Primary task two

Primary task three

Secondary tasks

If you could live this day again, what would you do differently this time?

What am I grateful for today?

Appointments

Hero on a Mission Daily Planner

Date

My Morning Ritual

- [ ] I've read my eulogy
- [ ] I've reviewed my vision worksheets
- [ ] I've reviewed my goals

Primary task one

Primary task two

Primary task three

Secondary tasks

- [ ]
- [ ]
- [ ]
- [ ]
- [ ]

If you could live this day again, what would you do differently this time?

-
-
-

What am I grateful for today?

-
-
-
-

Appointments

Hero on a Mission Daily Planner

Date

My Morning Ritual

- [ ] I've read my eulogy
- [ ] I've reviewed my vision worksheets
- [ ] I've reviewed my goals

Primary task one

Primary task two

Primary task three

Secondary tasks

- [ ]
- [ ]
- [ ]
- [ ]
- [ ]

If you could live this day again, what would you do differently this time?

-
-
-

What am I grateful for today?

-
-
-
-

Appointments

	:
	:
	:
	:
	:
	:
	:
	:
	:
	:
	:
	:
	:
	:

Hero on a Mission Daily Planner

Date

My Morning Ritual

- [ ] I've read my eulogy
- [ ] I've reviewed my vision worksheets
- [ ] I've reviewed my goals

Primary task one

Primary task two

Primary task three

Secondary tasks

- [ ]
- [ ]
- [ ]
- [ ]
- [ ]

If you could live this day again, what would you do differently this time?

•
•
•

What am I grateful for today?

•
•
•
•

Appointments

:
:
:
:
:
:
:
:
:
:
:
:
:

Hero on a Mission Daily Planner

Date

My Morning Ritual

- [ ] I've read my eulogy
- [ ] I've reviewed my vision worksheets
- [ ] I've reviewed my goals

Primary task one

Primary task two

Primary task three

Secondary tasks

- [ ]
- [ ]
- [ ]
- [ ]
- [ ]

If you could live this day again, what would you do differently this time?

What am I grateful for today?

Appointments

Hero on a Mission Daily Planner

Date

My Morning Ritual

- [ ] I've read my eulogy
- [ ] I've reviewed my vision worksheets
- [ ] I've reviewed my goals

Primary task one

Primary task two

Primary task three

Secondary tasks

- [ ]
- [ ]
- [ ]
- [ ]
- [ ]

If you could live this day again, what would you do differently this time?

-
-
-

What am I grateful for today?

-
-
-
-

Appointments

Hero on a Mission Daily Planner

Date

My Morning Ritual

- [ ] I've read my eulogy
- [ ] I've reviewed my vision worksheets
- [ ] I've reviewed my goals

Primary task one

Primary task two

Primary task three

Secondary tasks

- [ ]
- [ ]
- [ ]
- [ ]
- [ ]

If you could live this day again, what would you do differently this time?

-
-
-

What am I grateful for today?

-
-
-
-

Appointments

	:
	:
	:
	:
	:
	:
	:
	:
	:
	:
	:
	:
	:
	:

"When we perceive ourselves as weak and in need of a strong person to protect us, we are more likely to submit to a villain and serve them in order to associate with that strength. Minions believe if they are loyal to the villain, the villain will be loyal to them. This is almost never the case. Again, villains do not intimately connect with others. Villains use others."

From *Hero on a Mission*

THE DESIRE FOR a strongman to take care of us is a product of an inner weakness and a belief we cannot take care of ourselves.

Hero on a Mission Daily Planner

Date

My Morning Ritual

- [ ] I've read my eulogy
- [ ] I've reviewed my vision worksheets
- [ ] I've reviewed my goals

Primary task one

Primary task two

Primary task three

Secondary tasks

- [ ]
- [ ]
- [ ]
- [ ]
- [ ]

If you could live this day again, what would you do differently this time?

-
-
-

What am I grateful for today?

-
-
-
-

Appointments

Hero on a Mission Daily Planner

Date

My Morning Ritual

- [ ] I've read my eulogy
- [ ] I've reviewed my vision worksheets
- [ ] I've reviewed my goals

Primary task one

Primary task two

Primary task three

Secondary tasks

- [ ]
- [ ]
- [ ]
- [ ]
- [ ]

If you could live this day again, what would you do differently this time?

-
-
-

What am I grateful for today?

-
-
-
-

Appointments

	:
	:
	:
	:
	:
	:
	:
	:
	:
	:
	:
	:
	:

Hero on a Mission Daily Planner

Date

My Morning Ritual

- [ ] I've read my eulogy
- [ ] I've reviewed my vision worksheets
- [ ] I've reviewed my goals

Primary task one

Primary task two

Primary task three

Secondary tasks

- [ ]
- [ ]
- [ ]
- [ ]
- [ ]

If you could live this day again, what would you do differently this time?

-
-
-

What am I grateful for today?

-
-
-
-

Appointments

Hero on a Mission Daily Planner

Date

My Morning Ritual

- [ ] I've read my eulogy
- [ ] I've reviewed my vision worksheets
- [ ] I've reviewed my goals

Primary task one

Primary task two

Primary task three

Secondary tasks

- [ ]
- [ ]
- [ ]
- [ ]
- [ ]

If you could live this day again, what would you do differently this time?

What am I grateful for today?

Appointments

Hero on a Mission Daily Planner

Date

My Morning Ritual

- [ ] I've read my eulogy
- [ ] I've reviewed my vision worksheets
- [ ] I've reviewed my goals

Primary task one

Primary task two

Primary task three

Secondary tasks

- [ ]
- [ ]
- [ ]
- [ ]
- [ ]

If you could live this day again, what would you do differently this time?

-
-
-

What am I grateful for today?

-
-
-
-

Appointments

	:
	:
	:
	:
	:
	:
	:
	:
	:
	:
	:
	:
	:

Hero on a Mission Daily Planner

Date

My Morning Ritual

- [ ] I've read my eulogy
- [ ] I've reviewed my vision worksheets
- [ ] I've reviewed my goals

Primary task one

Primary task two

Primary task three

Secondary tasks

- [ ]
- [ ]
- [ ]
- [ ]
- [ ]

If you could live this day again, what would you do differently this time?

-
-
-

What am I grateful for today?

-
-
-
-

Appointments

Hero on a Mission Daily Planner

Date

My Morning Ritual

- [ ] I've read my eulogy
- [ ] I've reviewed my vision worksheets
- [ ] I've reviewed my goals

Primary task one

Primary task two

Primary task three

Secondary tasks

- [ ]
- [ ]
- [ ]
- [ ]
- [ ]

If you could live this day again, what would you do differently this time?

-
-
-

What am I grateful for today?

-
-
-
-

Appointments

The four characters that exist inside us are:

THE VICTIM

The one who believes they are helpless.

THE VILLAIN

The one who makes others small.

THE HERO

The one who accepts the challenge and transforms.

THE GUIDE

The one who helps others win.

From *Hero on a Mission*

THE FOUR MAJOR archetypes we find in stories don't exist in stories. Rather, each of them exists in every person, including you. To the degree we surface victim and villain energy, our lives deteriorate. To the degree we surface hero and guide energy, we will experience a deep sense of meaning.

Hero on a Mission Daily Planner

Date

My Morning Ritual

- [ ] I've read my eulogy
- [ ] I've reviewed my vision worksheets
- [ ] I've reviewed my goals

Primary task one

Primary task two

Primary task three

Secondary tasks

- [ ]
- [ ]
- [ ]
- [ ]
- [ ]

If you could live this day again, what would you do differently this time?

•
•
•

What am I grateful for today?

•
•
•
•

Appointments

:
:
:
:
:
:
:
:
:
:
:
:
:

Hero on a Mission Daily Planner

Date

My Morning Ritual

- [ ] I've read my eulogy
- [ ] I've reviewed my vision worksheets
- [ ] I've reviewed my goals

Primary task one

Primary task two

Primary task three

Secondary tasks

- [ ]
- [ ]
- [ ]
- [ ]
- [ ]

If you could live this day again, what would you do differently this time?

-
-
-

What am I grateful for today?

-
-
-
-

Appointments

Hero on a Mission Daily Planner

Date

My Morning Ritual

- [ ] I've read my eulogy
- [ ] I've reviewed my vision worksheets
- [ ] I've reviewed my goals

Primary task one

Primary task two

Primary task three

Secondary tasks

- [ ]
- [ ]
- [ ]
- [ ]
- [ ]

If you could live this day again, what would you do differently this time?

-
-
-

What am I grateful for today?

-
-
-
-

Appointments

	:
	:
	:
	:
	:
	:
	:
	:
	:
	:
	:
	:
	:
	:

Hero on a Mission Daily Planner

Date

My Morning Ritual

- [ ] I've read my eulogy
- [ ] I've reviewed my vision worksheets
- [ ] I've reviewed my goals

Primary task one

Primary task two

Primary task three

Secondary tasks

- [ ]
- [ ]
- [ ]
- [ ]
- [ ]

If you could live this day again, what would you do differently this time?

-
-
-

What am I grateful for today?

-
-
-
-

Appointments

Hero on a Mission Daily Planner

Date

My Morning Ritual

- [ ] I've read my eulogy
- [ ] I've reviewed my vision worksheets
- [ ] I've reviewed my goals

Primary task one

Primary task two

Primary task three

Secondary tasks

- [ ]
- [ ]
- [ ]
- [ ]
- [ ]

If you could live this day again, what would you do differently this time?

-
-
-

What am I grateful for today?

-
-
-
-

Appointments

Hero on a Mission Daily Planner

Date

My Morning Ritual

☐ I've read my eulogy

☐ I've reviewed my vision worksheets

☐ I've reviewed my goals

Primary task one

Primary task two

Primary task three

Secondary tasks

☐
☐
☐
☐
☐

If you could live this day again, what would you do differently this time?

•
•
•

What am I grateful for today?

•
•
•
•

Appointments

:
:
:
:
:
:
:
:
:
:
:
:
:

Hero on a Mission Daily Planner

Date

My Morning Ritual

- [ ] I've read my eulogy
- [ ] I've reviewed my vision worksheets
- [ ] I've reviewed my goals

Primary task one

Primary task two

Primary task three

Secondary tasks

- [ ]
- [ ]
- [ ]
- [ ]
- [ ]

If you could live this day again, what would you do differently this time?

-
-
-

What am I grateful for today?

-
-
-
-

Appointments

:
:
:
:
:
:
:
:
:
:
:
:
:

"Our tendency to see ourselves as victims—when in fact we are not—drains meaning from our lives by not allowing us to connect in healthy relationships. Healthy connection happens when two people enter into a mutually beneficial relationship. When you have something that makes me happy and I have something that makes you happy and we exchange those things, the relationship flourishes. But when we play the victim, we find ourselves taking more than we give."

From *Hero on a Mission*

WHEN WE SEE ourselves as victims, it's not just our stories that stall—our relationships suffer too.

Hero on a Mission Daily Planner

Date

My Morning Ritual

- [ ] I've read my eulogy
- [ ] I've reviewed my vision worksheets
- [ ] I've reviewed my goals

Primary task one

Primary task two

Primary task three

Secondary tasks

- [ ]
- [ ]
- [ ]
- [ ]
- [ ]

If you could live this day again, what would you do differently this time?

-
-
-

What am I grateful for today?

-
-
-
-

Appointments

Hero on a Mission Daily Planner

Date

My Morning Ritual

- [ ] I've read my eulogy
- [ ] I've reviewed my vision worksheets
- [ ] I've reviewed my goals

Primary task one

Primary task two

Primary task three

Secondary tasks

- [ ]
- [ ]
- [ ]
- [ ]
- [ ]

If you could live this day again, what would you do differently this time?

-
-
-

What am I grateful for today?

-
-
-
-

Appointments

Hero on a Mission Daily Planner

Date

My Morning Ritual

- [ ] I've read my eulogy
- [ ] I've reviewed my vision worksheets
- [ ] I've reviewed my goals

Primary task one

Primary task two

Primary task three

Secondary tasks

- [ ]
- [ ]
- [ ]
- [ ]
- [ ]

If you could live this day again, what would you do differently this time?

-
-
-

What am I grateful for today?

-
-
-
-

Appointments

	:
	:
	:
	:
	:
	:
	:
	:
	:
	:
	:
	:
	:
	:

Hero on a Mission Daily Planner

Date

My Morning Ritual

- [ ] I've read my eulogy
- [ ] I've reviewed my vision worksheets
- [ ] I've reviewed my goals

Primary task one

Primary task two

Primary task three

Secondary tasks

- [ ]
- [ ]
- [ ]
- [ ]
- [ ]

If you could live this day again, what would you do differently this time?

What am I grateful for today?

Appointments

Hero on a Mission Daily Planner

Date

My Morning Ritual

- [ ] I've read my eulogy
- [ ] I've reviewed my vision worksheets
- [ ] I've reviewed my goals

Primary task one

Primary task two

Primary task three

Secondary tasks

- [ ]
- [ ]
- [ ]
- [ ]
- [ ]

If you could live this day again, what would you do differently this time?

-
-
-

What am I grateful for today?

-
-
-
-

Appointments

Hero on a Mission Daily Planner

Date

My Morning Ritual

- [ ] I've read my eulogy
- [ ] I've reviewed my vision worksheets
- [ ] I've reviewed my goals

Primary task one

Primary task two

Primary task three

Secondary tasks

- [ ]
- [ ]
- [ ]
- [ ]
- [ ]

If you could live this day again, what would you do differently this time?

-
-
-

What am I grateful for today?

-
-
-
-

Appointments

:
:
:
:
:
:
:
:
:
:
:
:
:

Hero on a Mission Daily Planner

Date

My Morning Ritual

- [ ] I've read my eulogy
- [ ] I've reviewed my vision worksheets
- [ ] I've reviewed my goals

Primary task one

Primary task two

Primary task three

Secondary tasks

- [ ]
- [ ]
- [ ]
- [ ]
- [ ]

If you could live this day again, what would you do differently this time?

What am I grateful for today?

Appointments

"I don't think any of us should trust fate to write the story of our lives. Fate is a terrible writer."

From *Hero on a Mission*

THERE ARE A myriad of ways we tend to trust fate with our lives. But I believe fate is entirely neutral. It is neither for you nor against you. Mostly, fate is a blank canvas on which we paint. We blame our problems on fate and our successes too. But an external locus of control leads to ruin. We have far more control over our lives than we believe. For the next few months I'll be sharing quotes from my new book. The journey from trusting fate to accepting agency over my story has been the most helpful journey of my life. I might even call it a universal spiritual quest.

Goal name	Completion date

Describe this goal

Why does this goal matter to you?

Goal partners *(optional)*	1	2	3
Milestones	1	2	3

Daily sacrifices

Repetition record

Goal name	Completion date

Describe this goal

Why does this goal matter to you?

Goal partners *(optional)*	1	2	3

Milestones	1	2	3

Daily sacrifices

Repetition record

Goal name	Completion date

Describe this goal

Why does this goal matter to you?

Goal partners *(optional)*	1	2	3
Milestones	1	2	3

Daily sacrifices

Repetition record

Goal name	Completion date

Describe this goal

Why does this goal matter to you?

Goal partners *(optional)*	1	2	3

Milestones	1	2	3

Daily sacrifices

Repetition record

Goal name	Completion date

Describe this goal

Why does this goal matter to you?

Goal partners *(optional)*	1	2	3
Milestones	1	2	3

Daily sacrifices

Repetition record												

Goal name	Completion date

Describe this goal

Why does this goal matter to you?

Goal partners *(optional)*	1	2	3
Milestones	1	2	3

Daily sacrifices

Repetition record

Goal name	Completion date

Describe this goal

Why does this goal matter to you?

Goal partners *(optional)*	1	2	3
Milestones	1	2	3

Daily sacrifices

Repetition record												

Goal name	Completion date

Describe this goal

Why does this goal matter to you?

Goal partners *(optional)*	1	2	3

Milestones	1	2	3

Daily sacrifices

Repetition record												

About the Author

DONALD MILLER is the CEO of *Business Made Simple* and the author of ten books, including *Building a StoryBrand* and *Blue Like Jazz*. He and his wife, Betsy, along with their daughter, Emmeline, live in Nashville, Tennessee.

To take a deep dive into more Hero on a Mission resources, scan the QR code below: